Creative Painting with Tempera

Ia. Strange Creatures of the Deep Sea.
Painting by 13-year-old girl.

Ib. Children of Candy Land.
Painting by 13-year-old girl.

Ic. Village of the Little People.   Painting by 14-year-old girl.

Pauline Albenda

Creative Painting with Tempera

A Guide to Developmental Learning in Painting

VNR VAN NOSTRAND REINHOLD COMPANY
New York   Cincinnati   Toronto   London   Melbourne

To the boys and girls in the
New York City public schools

Acknowledgments

The idea for this book was initiated by Sterling McIlhany, editor, who assisted me through its early stages. Nancy Newman provided further able assistance with the manuscript. Many of the thoughts expressed are the result of a long association with my friends and colleagues, Filomena Bruno and Helen Zeller, who fostered a teaching atmosphere of innovation and experimentation. They also made available to me many of the original paintings used as illustrations. The paintings were done by boys and girls in grades 7, 8, and 9 under regular classroom conditions. Si Drabkin, a sensitive photographer, produced the fine photographs of the children's paintings. My appreciation is given to The Metropolitan Museum of Art, New York City, for permission to reproduce paintings in their collection. I am obliged to the Real Academia de Bellas Artes, Madrid, for allowing me to illustrate the fresco shown in Figure 7.

Van Nostrand Reinhold Company Regional Offices:
New York, Cincinnati, Chicago, Millbrae, Dallas.
Van Nostrand Reinhold Company Foreign Offices:
London, Toronto, Melbourne.

Copyright © 1970 by Reinhold Book Corporation.
Library of Congress Catalog Card No. 70-110055.

Published by Van Nostrand Reinhold Company,
450 West 33rd Street, New York, N. Y. 10001.

Designed by Jean Callan King.
Printed by Halliday Lithograph Corporation.
Color printed by Bridge Litho Company, Incorporated.
Bound by Publishers Book Bindery, Incorporated.

15 14 13 12 11 10 9 8 7 6 5 4 3 2 1

Contents

Introduction   6

1. History of Tempera Painting   7

2. Preparation of Painting Materials   14

3. Elements of Design and Color Principles   16
Unit 1. Lines and shapes / Unit 2. Line, Shape, and Color /
Unit 3. Arrangement of Line, Shape and Color / Unit 4. Combining Colors /
Unit 5. Color Spectrum / Unit 6. White and Black / Unit 7. Movement in Space /
Unit 8. Painting Styles / Unit 9. Organization Through Color, Design
and Movement

4. Communication and Vision in Design   38
Unit 1. Creating a Mood or Feeling / Unit 2. Painting to Music /
Unit 3. Interpretation Through Design / Unit 4. Imagination and Invention /
Unit 5. Discovering Subject Matter in Design / Unit 6. Atmosphere of a Scene /
Unit 7. Painting a Theme in Design / Unit 8. Imaginative Points of View

5. Human Figures in Painting   54
Unit 1. Human Structure / Unit 2. Observed Single Poses /
Unit 3. Figure Grouping / Unit 4. Human Figures in a Setting /
Unit 5. Human Figures in Activities / Unit 6. Themes Emphasizing
the Human Figure / Unit 7. Self-Portrait

6. Nature   78
Unit 1. Landscapes and Seascapes / Unit 2. Cityscapes / Unit 3. Nature's Seasons /
Unit 4. Plant Life / Unit 5. Animal Life / Unit 6. Still-Life

7. Learning Through Visual Aids   94

Introduction

As a teacher who is concerned with the artistic efforts of young people, I am constantly amazed by the immensity and vitality inherent in the creative scope of youth. Yet, I believe that this capacity for personal expression needs an incentive to enliven and intensify the inner urge to create through art, a force that may too easily remain hidden from recognition.

Fundamental for any prolonged study with art activities is the inclusion of painting. Painting, notably with the flexible medium of tempera, can lead adolescents and young adults to discover the importance of such elements as color, line, pattern, rhythm, and spatial relationships on a two-dimensional surface. Once the young person is introduced to the tempera medium, the ease with which it can be manipulated will increase his confidence. His timidity will diminish as his ability to express himself coherently expands.

Through an ordered course of study in painting, the student can develop an insight into the meaning of that world we term "art," for art experiences that proceed along casual lines are less apt to achieve whatever creative sensibilities may be sought. It seems, then, more reasonable to formulate a sequence of art studies whose content will heighten both the learning process and the facility to communicate new, exciting, personal statements. Through his experiences with tempera painting, the youthful person will become aware that art expression involves a combining of factors interacting with one another, resulting in the transformation of the original ingredients into new modes of expression. What are these underlying factors that are so essential for a fuller meaning in the performance of art activities? Briefly, they consist of the process of perceiving, understanding, experiencing, and expressing.

This book, then, is written for those who have been seeking guidelines in planning a program of tempera painting for young people—a program of both education and expression.

1 History of Tempera Painting

The presentation of the history of painting provides a suitable introduction. It will demonstrate that throughout the far-reaching period of man's artistic efforts painting has been foremost as a mode of creativity.

Below is a brief description of the history of painting—confined to the medium of tempera—which will furnish a framework for study. The summary follows the method of historical continuity, beginning with earliest times and including our present era. This is but one possible means to introduce the subject. Other approaches may be initiated. By comparing and contrasting select examples, one may view painting as an expression of man's beliefs, ideals, ideas. Or, the history of painting may be studied primarily as the illustration of different times and societies.

Painting as an art medium has a tradition that extends far back into prehistory. It was employed to depict images and symbols, usually of a religious nature, and to record events pertaining to daily life. The numerous works of art that still survive from the Stone Age and, particularly, from the ancient world attest to the variety of styles of painting and the uses they were put to.

Paleolithic art (about 15,000-10,000 B.C.) is exemplified by cave paintings such as those discovered at Altamira in northern Spain and at La Mouthe, Font de Gaume, Les Combarelles, and Lascaux in the Dordogne region of France. Most often depicted upon the cavern walls were marvelously drawn animal forms dominated by boldness of line and color, which was limited to red, red-brown, and black pigments. When man eventually turned to settled communities, he did not hesitate to practice the art of wall painting for decorating the interiors of houses and shrines. This is shown by recent excavations of early settlements in central Turkey (about 7000-5500 B.C.), which reveal a well-established tradition of painting.

With the emergence of recorded history (about 3100 B.C.), the artist became more knowledge-

1. Wall painting: Apuy and his wife receiving offerings. Egyptian, XIX Dynasty. (The Metropolitan Museum of Art)

able in the use of materials and in the techniques of painting. He was able to manipulate the medium to satisfy whatever demands were imposed upon him. For the painters of ancient Egypt and the Near East, all efforts were devoted primarily to the decoration of ceilings and walls of royal tombs, temples, and palaces. Scenes in Egyptian paintings often proclaim secular events surrounding the life of the Pharaoh (Figure 1), although there were also included themes having religious significance. Often a sense of elegance and grace

permeates these paintings. The paintings reveal, too, the sensitive manner in which the Egyptian artist depicted the wonders of the natural world (Figure 2). While comparatively little painted decoration has survived in Mesopotamia, indications are that room interiors of the elaborate structures of Babylonia and Assyria were embellished with bold, geometric designs, occasionally combined with representations of human figures and other naturalistic forms.

The painting medium used throughout the

ancient world consisted of tempera, a mixture composed of color pigments extracted from minerals, egg yolk used as an adhesive, and water to liquefy the paint. The distinctive qualities of this medium, which permits the placing of one layer upon another, are its opacity, produced by repeated coats of a single tone; its opalescence, produced by painting lighter tones over a dark, single tone; its transparency, produced by painting darker tones over a lighter, single tone. The surface to be painted upon was often prepared with a thin coating of plaster or gesso. The easiest method of working was to apply the paints to the dry surface, a technique sometimes described as *fresco secco*. In later periods, the tempera was applied upon the gesso while it was still wet, a technique that made greater demands upon the artist. This method is known as true fresco. Frequently the paintings were done in fresco and then retouched in *secco*. Decorating wall surfaces with fresco paintings became more prominent in time, and examples of this style of painting are known throughout the Roman, Byzantine, Romanesque, and Renaissance periods.

2. Wall painting: Fowling scene (detail). Egyptian, XII Dynasty. (The Metropolitan Museum of Art)

3. Wall painting from Boscoreale. Roman, first century B.C. (The Metropolitan Museum of Art, Rogers Fund, 1903)

9

The most noteworthy paintings of the Roman period are those unearthed at Herculaneum and Pompeii, the cities buried by the great eruption of Vesuvius in 79 A.D. The finds of mural art in Pompeii offer a complete survey of two centuries of Greco-Roman painting. The artistic tastes revealed in the paintings are exceptional and range from the use of architectural perspective for purposes of decoration (Figure 3, on preceding page) to complex figure compositions illustrating scenes of ancient mythology.

The monastic art that typifies the painting of the Byzantine period (about 700-1450 A.D.) is generally identified with the frescoes found in the churches and monasteries of the Eastern Mediterranean. Closely allied with mural paintings are small panel paintings, also made with the tempera medium (Figure 4). Wood panels consisting

4. Triptych. Deesis with St. George and St. Demetrius of Thessalonica. Greco-Italian painter, unknown, 16th century. (The Metropolitan Museum of Art, Gift of Mrs. Henry Morgenthau, 1933)

Parallel with the development of Byzantine art in the East was the rise and growth of Islam. The artists of Muslim art sought the medium of tempera to illuminate manuscripts and books conspicuous for their delicate and jewel-like treatment (Figure 5).

The traditional use of tempera for mural and panel painting continued in Western Europe during the Romanesque period, but it was in Italy that the medium was given new impetus in the matter of representation. The transition into a renewed creative activity, which was begun quietly in the thirteenth and fourteenth centuries by such masters as the Florentine Giotto (about 1276-1337) and the Sienese painters Duccio di Buoninsegna (about 1255-1318) and Simone Martini (about 1284-1344), finally attained its greatest achievement in the Quattrocento and early part of the Cinquecento. The inception of the Early Renaissance, marked by the frescoes of Masaccio (1401-1428), brought a new spirit into the art that flourished in the century that followed (Figure 6), culminating in the paintings of Michelangelo (1475-1564), particularly his ceiling fresco of the Sistine Chapel and the *Last Judgment*.

5 (above). Portrait of a woman. Persian, Safavid Period, mid-16th century. (The Metropolitan Museum of Art, Purchase, 1952, Joseph Pulitzer Bequest)

6 (right). *Journey of the Magi* by Sassetta (Stefano di Giovanni). Italian, Sienese, 1392–1450. (The Metropolitan Museum of Art, Bequest of Maitland F. Griggs, 1943)

variously of hard pine, olive, nut tree, poplar, or plane served as the ground, and, although the methods of preparing the panels differed widely, the real variations detected in the techniques of Byzantine painting were provided by new combinations of color.

With the introduction of paints possessing an oil base—an event that occurred during the fifteenth century in Flanders—by such masters as the brothers Hubert (died 1426) and Jan van Eyck (died 1441) and Rogier van der Weyden (1399-1464), tempera painting gradually lost its prominence as the medium for making major works of art and was superseded by oil painting, which remains the prevalent painting material to the

7 *(left)*. Detail: ceiling fresco by Francisco de Goya y Lucientes. Spanish. (Real Academia de San Fernando)

8 *(below)*. *A Crow Flew By* by Andrew Wyeth. American. (The Metropolitan Museum of Art, Arthur H. Hearn Fund, 1950)

9 *(facing page)*. *Broadway* by Mark George Tobey. American. (The Metropolitan Museum of Art, Arthur H. Hearn Fund, 1942)

present day. Tempera was still retained, however, particularly for large wall decorations by such noteworthy artists as the Venetian Tiepolo (1696-1770), renowned for his fresco decorations, and the Spaniard Goya (1746-1828), who painted the frescoes of the cupola of S. Antonio de la Florida in Madrid (Figure 7).

At the turn of this century, fresco painting for huge murals was revived by a school of Mexican artists, which included, among others, José Orozco (1883-1949) and Diego Rivera (1886-1957). The subjects of their murals show the influence of politics in their homeland. In recent years a few artists have returned to tempera painting as the medium for their works. Among the more important artists are the Americans Ben Shahn (1898-1969) and Andrew Wyeth (born 1917). While the paintings of the former artist are often flat and poster-like, tending toward subjects dealing with social criticism, the realism revealed in the latter's works adopts an illustrative technique that strives for a more personal art (Figure 8). Another American artist, Mark Tobey (born 1890), has employed a more relaxed, spontaneous effect in the use of tempera for his paintings (Figure 9).

To what extent tempera painting will be practiced in the future remains uncertain. Its distinctive characteristics have enabled tempera to survive the era of oil painting, a medium which in turn appears to be in competition with a newer medium, acrylics. Notable for tempera is the ease with which it can be manipulated and the many uses to which it can be put, even when combined with other materials (such as wax to produce encaustic). One may suppose, then, that tempera painting will continue to attract the attention of artists, thus assuring the medium a place in the future development of painting.

Suggested Reading for the Student:

Holme, Bryan (ed.). *Pictures to Live With*. The Viking Press, New York.

Jacobs, David. *Master Painters of the Renaissance*. The Viking Press, New York.

Janson, H. W. and Janson, Dora Jane. *The History of Painting for Young People*. Harry N. Abrams, Inc., New York.

Willard, Charlotte. *What Is a Masterpiece?* G. P. Putnam's Sons, New York.

2 Preparation of Painting Materials

Basic for a prolonged study of painting with tempera is the assembling of art materials, each of which serves a specific function. Several items can be used and re-used many times if properly maintained. Other materials can be shared conveniently among small groups of students. Because of this, be certain to emphasize that co-operation involving the care and maintenance of art materials is a must.

Paints. Tempera paints, as described in the previous chapter, are water-soluble and may be obtained commercially in powder form, in semi-moist cakes, or in liquid form. When working with large groups of students, it is advantageous to prepare the pigments for use in a semi-thick liquid state, since this allows for greater flexibility in application. Tempera paints can then be kept conveniently in small plastic or glass jars with wide openings, preferably of the same size (I have found baby-food jars suitable for this purpose). The small jars should be used for all painting activities. There are several reasons for this: smaller jars are less cumbersome to work from; in the event of accidents, wastage will be minimal; maintenance procedures will be more efficient. When not in use, the jars should be covered to avoid hardening of the pigments.

For those planning a program of painting on a limited budget, it is recommended that the range of colors be limited to the primary and secondary colors, white, and black. These eight colors will furnish the essential needs, since a variety of other colors can be made through mixing. Also, with too many colors to choose from, the student may become confused with his selections.

Brushes. These come in an assortment of types and widths, varying from 1/16 of an inch to 1 inch. Several sizes and types of brushes should be made available. Flat bristle brushes are effective for producing broad, freely applied strokes. Round brushes with tapered points are suitable for line and detail work. Start the students working with the larger brushes. This will encourage freedom of expression. Later, include the smaller brushes for detail work.

Paper. Newsprint and drawing papers, 19 x 22 inches, are ideal for painting upon. Tempera will dry quickly when applied to these papers. Avoid cutting the paper into smaller sections, since this may result in a tightness of style in the art work due to a diminished painting area. Experiment with other types of paper, too, such as newspaper, wrapping paper, tissue paper.

Water Containers. Large, empty coffee or fruit cans make satisfactory water containers as well as providing storage for brushes. Brighten their appearance by painting the cans with colored, enamel paints. This will also deter any process of rusting resulting from continued contact with water.

Mixing Cups. Small plastic dishes (3½ inches in diameter) make suitable containers for mixing the color pigments. When clean and dry, they can be stacked easily. Similar-type metal dishes can also be used, but these have a tendency to rust.

Sponges, Paper Towels, Old Newspapers. It is advisable to have a handy supply of these items available. They can be utilized for clean-up purposes. The tops of tables and easels (if used) should be covered with old newspapers to protect their surfaces from unnecessary markings. Sponges and towels can serve to clean brushes, paint jars, and mixing cups, as well as other clean-up uses.

Trays. This item is ideal for the handling of individual paint set-ups comprising paint jars, water containers, brushes, and other materials. It also facilitates the transporting of the art materials in the art room.

3 Elements of Design and Color Principles

This section introduces the basic elements and principles of design through experimentation and discovery. Each unit focuses upon a single aspect of learning. The organization of the units is arranged to provide a sequence, advancing from the simplest to more complex projects. This will permit proper attention to be given to each of the many components of design and properties of color. Furthermore, each topic in this chapter, as in the other sections, is intended to be broad enough to allow for modification, according to the judgment of the teacher.

An additional aspect of this chapter is to furnish the student with opportunities to master the tools and techniques of the tempera medium. We believe that the development of skills should be real and not contrived; we avoid emphasis upon any technique of painting that may impede individuality of style. It is desirable to have the introductory activities studied in sequence to stimulate confidence in the ability of the young person to succeed. Remember: allow each student to progress at his own pace. Soon he will find that he can paint with ease while nurturing a style of his own. The time devoted to each painting unit should vary, therefore, to satisfy the special needs of the student.

Unit 1.
Lines and Shapes

Basic experiences are explored with lines and shapes. (Figures 10 and 11)

Before commencing upon the first of many painting lessons to come, prepare the art materials in a manner which is appropriate for the classroom situation. We suggest that the choice of colors for this and the following series of activities be limited to red, yellow, blue, orange, violet, and green. There are two reasons for this: one is that the youngster will not be confused by having to

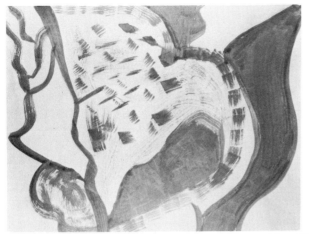

choose from an excessive amount of colors, and the other is that the colors white and black will be presented in separate units of study.

This introductory exercise will present, in the simplest way, the basic elements in a painting. These elements are line, shape, and color. The primary concern at this time is to give encouragement to the student and lead him to discover the meaning of these elements for himself. The simplest approach is to limit the choice of colors to any one of the available colors.

10. Lines and Shapes in Orange

11. Lines and Shapes in Red

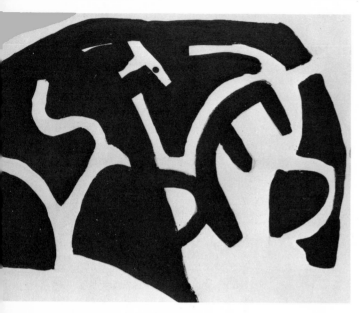

12. Lines and Shapes in Yellow and Blue

Select a color. Dip the brush into the jar of paint, and make a stroke upon the surface of the paper. Make another stroke. Try a long stroke. Have it curve, turn, twist; change its width. Alter the direction: horizontal, oblique, vertical. Repeat the direction several times. Fill in some of the unpainted portions of the paper and leave other sections untouched.

What has been created in the painting are lines and shapes made with color.

Unit 2.
Line, Shape, and Color

The relationships of line, shape, and color are discovered through their application. (Figure 12)

In this exercise the separate elements of line, shape, and color are brought together in a single painting. At this time, increase the choice of colors to two to initiate color relationships.

Now is the occasion for guiding the student towards an awareness of the need for making decisions as he attempts to relate the parts of the surface to produce a painting that is visually pleasing. While he works, important discoveries can be made. It is exciting when a youngster finds new elements of design through his painting experiences. Be quick to give definition to these discoveries. For example, a series of dots or small lines makes a pattern; painted areas that are different in size and color are said to have variety; pigments applied with a dry brush give texture.

Painting Activity
Select any two colors. Paint with one color, making large, sweeping strokes across the surface, or

II. County Fair. Painting by 15-year-old girl.

else do a series of short, repetitive movements. Clean the brush, and then continue painting with the second color chosen. Remember: do not repaint any part of the paper. The two pure colors must remain unmixed; they touch but do not overlap. Become aware of the area to be covered. Make lines and shapes similar to form a pattern, or make them different to create variety through color, size, and contour. Cover the entire surface of the paper with tempera.

Unit 3.
Arrangement of Line, Shape, and Color

The attention given to careful selection and placement of lines, shapes, and colors will lead to pleasing effects (Figures 13-18)

Further attention is given to the manner in which the painting is evolved and completed. Challenge the student to plan a painting whose elements are carefully interrelated to form an attractive, unified whole. There are several points that may be singled out as guidelines for determining the direction that the painting will take to completion. First, the entire surface of the paper is to be considered as the area to be painted upon. Second, to increase interest in the appearance of the painting, some lines, shapes, and colors will be more or less emphasized.

This unit can be divided into two parts and explained in the ways suggested.

13. Arrangement in Red, Yellow, and Blue

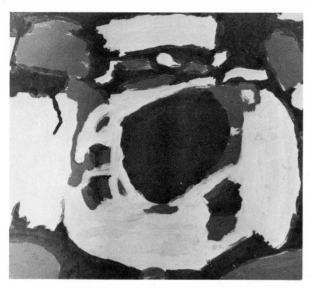

14. Arrangement in Green, Yellow, and Blue

15. Arrangement in Green, Yellow, and Blue

Painting Activity

Part A (Figures 13-15). Limit the choice of colors to three. Begin to paint with pure, unmixed colors. Look at the painting as it develops, and realize that our eyes travel across the surface of the paper as they follow a color, line, or shape. Find ways in which a sense of movement can be achieved through the effective distribution of colors or through the rhythmical repetition of lines and shapes to produce patterns.

Plan to make one color more important than the others. This color may cover a greater portion of the surface, or it may attract our attention more frequently. When this occurs, the important color is defined as the predominant color, while the others are the subordinate colors.

Be inventive. Apply the color pigments with a dry brush, or wet the paper and then apply the colors. Observe the textural changes that result. Try other methods of achieving unexpected results.

Part B (Figures 16-18). Take this a step further. Select as many colors as desired. Create a painting that has variety of lines, shapes, patterns, and textures. As the painting progresses, remember that it should convey an interesting appearance and sense of excitement through color selection, placement of lines and shapes, and inventiveness.

Try to answer the following questions: Is there unity in the painting; that is, do its many parts seem to belong together? How does the painting appear? Can it be described as bold, lively, slow-moving, orderly, quiet?

16 *(facing page)*, 17 *(above)*, 18 *(above right).* Arrangements with Many Pure Colors

19. Many Pure and Mixed Colors

Unit 4.
Combining Colors

New results are achieved when colors are combined and mixed. (Figures 19-21)

The discovery to be made in this experience is that the attributes of color will alter when they are mixed with one another. Elicit from the student basic observations when comparing pure and mixed colors. A pure, unmixed color—now defined as hue—can be described as appearing brilliant. Show that the brilliance of a hue will lessen when other hues are combined with it. Point out, too, that with the introduction of mixed hues in a painting, color will appear less intense and more dull.

20. Combining Colors: Blue and Yellow

21. Combining Colors: Blue, Yellow, and Orange

Painting Activity

Select any two pure colors. Cover a portion of the paper surface with one color. Do the same with the second color. Mix a small amount of each color together in the dish, and apply the mixture to the paper. Increase the proportion of the mixture, and cover another area of the paper.

Try to alter a part of the painting by placing one color directly over another. Overlap one pure color over another; place a mixed color over a pure color; mix previously mixed colors.

Respond to the following questions: How do pure hues differ from mixed hues? Yes, the pure hues appear stronger and more brilliant. How are hues affected when mixed with one another? The more they are mixed in even proportions, the less is their intensity and brilliance.

Unit 5.
Color Spectrum

There is a realization that hues possess properties that can be established on a color scale. (Figures 22, 23)

In studying hue, we find that color is continuous on a disc or spectrum. By isolating color at regular points around the circle, certain facts can be discovered which make it easier to understand and use color. The division of hues may be made as follows: primary colors—the colors that are the basis for the mixing of all other colors; secondary colors—the colors that are the mixture of two primary colors. Each hue also has its complement or opposite color. The addition of a complementary color will make a hue duller or neutral in appearance.

These learnings should be made after the student has experimented with hues in a painting. The lesson can be controlled by limiting the number of colors upon the tray to the three primary colors: red, yellow, blue. The desired results will occur with assurance.

Painting Activity

Select two or three colors. Create a painting that demonstrates what has been learned previously. Combine and arrange in an interesting design pure and mixed hues, areas of colors, shapes, and lines.

Discover the observations that can be made when certain colors are mixed together:
• Red and yellow make orange.
• Yellow and blue make green.
• Blue and red make violet.

25

22, 23. Color Spectrum: Red, Yellow, and Blue

We learn that red, yellow, and blue are known as the primary colors. We learn that orange, green, and violet are known as the secondary colors.

Become alert to the properties of primary colors. See that red hues produce a quality of warmth and power. See that blue hues produce a quality of coolness and depth. See that yellow hues produce a quality of brilliance and light.

Unit 6.
White and Black

Color appearances are altered by introducing white and black. (Figures 24-28)

White and black possess properties different from other colors, which merit attention. They do not form part of the color spectrum. The significance of white and black is the effect achieved when these colors are mixed with hues or with one another. White will change the value of a hue to produce a tint; that is, a light value. Black will change the value of a hue to produce a shade; that is, a dark value. When white and black are used alone, they will produce a gray color, described as neutral. The gray color will be lighter or darker according to the amount of white or black used in the mixture. A painting that consists of a mixture of white and black only is called monochromatic.

In this unit the painting activity may be divided into two parts. Try them both for fuller results in learning the importance of white and black as colors.

Limit the selection of colors to white and black, plus the primary colors.

Painting Activity

Part A (Figures 24, 25). Use white and black only. This will result in a painting known as monochrome. By retaining white and black as pure colors, strong contrasts of light and dark can be achieved. Soften the areas of monochromatic color by mixing to produce gray. Make many grays ranging from white to black.

24, 25. Monochrome: Black and White

Part B (Figures 26-28). Begin another painting. Introduce one color plus white and black.

Observe the effects produced when white is added to color. The new color variations are described as *tints* of color. Observe the effects produced when black is added to color. The new color variations are described as *shades* of color.

Strive for strong, dramatic effects by increasing the importance of black in the mixture of colors. Or strive for rich, light effects by increasing the importance of white in the mixture of colors. Or strive for a balance of strength and lightness by using black and white in even proportions to combine gray tones with shades and tints of color.

26. Black, White, and Red

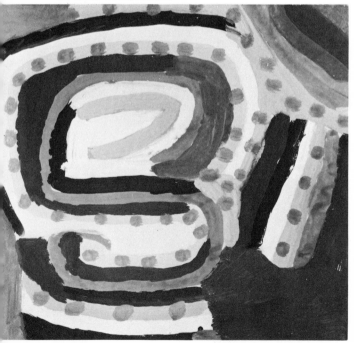

27. Black, White, Blue, and Red   28. White, Blue, and Yellow

Unit 7.
Movement in Space

A sense of spatial movement is achieved with forms that appear to advance and recede. (Figures 29, 30)

This exercise explores the appearance of objects in space, the limitless area in which all things move. As forms travel through the spatial field, they seem to have new aspects of identity. The student is guided to learn what these phenomena are by using his vision and understanding of spatial motion. The application of this knowledge

29. Near and Far: Spatial Explosion

30. Near and Far: Wheel in Motion

in painting will strengthen the student's ability to express motions that are rhythmical, dynamic, or agitating.

Painting Activity

Begin by making basic observations regarding objects in space:

What appears to happen to an object—such as a box—the further away or nearer to us it is placed? (Apparent change of size)

What happens to an object when a second object is placed in front of it? Behind it? (Partial view or full view)

Which of two objects attracts immediate attention, one that is colored red or one that is colored gray? (Strong or neutral hue)

We learn that while the surface of a painting is always flat, some forms can be made to appear near to the viewer while other forms can be made to appear distant. They may be described as advancing or receding. Now apply these observations in a painting.

Part A. Create a painting that conveys a sense of space and depth and distance by introducing forms that appear near or far. Experiment to achieve this affect by changing the size of shapes, overlapping shapes, altering intensities of hues, including color contrast, and using pattern and texture for detailed areas.

Part B. Try a new approach. Create a new mixed color, and cover the entire surface of the paper with that color. This color represents the spatial area through which lines and shapes appear to move forward, backward, diagonally, or sideways. When developing the painting, consider themes that describe the quality of spatial movement:

Oncoming masses.	Distant storms.
Swirling sands.	Rushing winds.
Flowing substance.	Surging waves.

Unit 8.
Painting Styles

Painting techniques are explored to increase the spontaneity of style. (Figures 31-33)

This section is directed towards stimulating greater freedom in the techniques of tempera painting. Often, there is a tendency on the part of the student to work in a rigid manner. This occurs when we find that edges are always carefully delineated and when there is a hesitancy to create new forms by obliviating, entirely or partially, lines and shapes that were previously painted. The goal, then, is to find the means to increase confidence in making changes through a more relaxed, spontaneous painterly style.

31. Painting with Areas of Color

Painting Activity

Consider the definition of "shape" and "area" of color. For purposes of clarification, we may define a "shape" as a form that is delineated by a specific outline, whether the shape is geometric (like a square) or irregular. An "area" of color, while it does have an edge, is less easy to mark off because of the extreme irregularity of its contour. This is called an amorphic form.

Think of specific examples. A regular shape may be round, may wiggle, may expand and contract but it has a definite beginning and end. Regarding an amorphic form, think of the movement of the ever-changing clouds, the sweeping waves of the sea as they turn into white foam, the windswept ripples of a running stream, or the spiraling smoke emerging from a chimney.

Create a painting that has no definite shapes or lines. To achieve this, try the following: use sweeping brush strokes. These may be short and placed one next to the other to form larger areas or long, single movements of varied lengths. Overlap areas of color with new areas to increase the sensation of movement.

Or try this approach: Soak the paper with water. While it is still wet, apply the pigments freely. Observe how colors expand and flow into one another. Increase interest by combining loosely applied strokes of color with free-flowing washes of color.

Compare the finished painting with an earlier example. It is now possible to distinguish the essential difference between them. Spontaneity of movement has grown in the most recent one.

32, 33. Painting with Areas of Color

Unit 9.
Organization Through
Color, Design, and Movement

There are many elements that contribute to a well-organized painting. (Figures 34-36)

We have explored the elements which comprise a painting—its line, shape, color, and style. The

34. Organization Through Elements of Design and Movement

35. Organization Through Elements of Design and Movement

constitute design and then discern how these features are interrelated in a painting. An outgrowth of this will be to promote, on the part of the student, an effort in planning and decision making, leading to sensitive use of perception and evaluation.

Painting Activity

Do a painting that shows what has been discovered in earlier painting lessons and reveals an understanding of the following attributes of a well-organized painting:

Variety. Achieve interest in the painting by introducing unexpected changes of hues, lines, shapes, and areas. Arrange forms in new directions and relationships. Display rhythmical repetition and pattern; alter their size and contour.

Value of color intensities. Colors, shapes, and areas can become more or less important, depending on their intensity and their reaction to one another in relation to their position in the painting.

Balance. A painting that is balanced should appear to "hold together." Placement of hues, lines, and shapes should complement one another so that there is a sense of unity in the whole painting. The painting can be filled with movement (dynamic) or display an orderly arrangement of those elements that contribute to its design (stability).

Center of interest. One section of the painting may appear more important than the other parts. It can be a shape, a hue, several shapes or several hues, a small part of the painting or a large part of the painting. Attention to the center of interest is directed by the other portions of the painting through the device of color contrast, careful placement of shapes and areas of color, and accents of lines.

task that remains is to understand the ways in which the many parts are brought together into a unified whole to produce a structured or well-designed painting. In order to achieve this, we must first separate and identify the features that

36. Organization Through Elements of Design and Movement

4 Communication and Vision in Design

The student who has acquired the basic skills of painting and has learned what constitutes the elements of design is prepared to apply his mastery for making visual statements in a personal manner. The capacity to think and feel resides within each individual. Through the medium of tempera painting vivid thoughts can be communicated and feelings can be depicted with conviction.

This chapter of study is planned to provide a sequence of painting activities that foster opportunities for self-expression. Moreover, subjects originating from external sources are given consideration, as they furnish the means for expanding the creative visions of the young individual.

Unit 1.
Creating a Mood or Feeling

Color, line, and shape are expressive and can convey a specific emotion or mood. (Figures 37, 38)

The student is urged to use the elements of color, line, and shape as the vehicle for making statements that are intimate and deeply felt. He will find that emotions can be conveyed in a painting with directness and excitement. To achieve these results, the student must select sentiments that are explicit.

37. Expressing a Feeling: Force and Strength

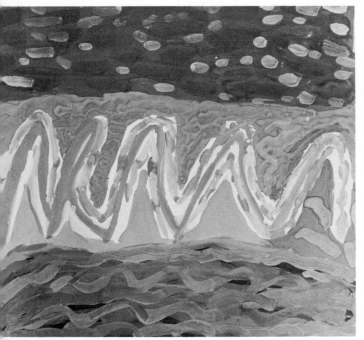

38. Expressing an Emotion: Wandering Alone

39. Response to Musical Sounds

Painting Activity

Words are expressive: fear, hate, loneliness, cheer, excitement, happiness, love, spiritual wonder. There are many more.

Colors possess expressive qualities. They can be described as warm or cool, light or dark, hard or soft, strong or weak, somber or cheerful, gentle or violent.

Selective combinations of colors and words can produce specific feelings or moods. Make a painting that denotes a personal mood or feeling. Start with expressions that stimulate the emotions, that encourage interpretations, that lead to personal statements which evoke immediate impact upon the viewer. Utilize colors that are most effective in describing the mood chosen and develop design qualities which heighten the theme of the painting. Each painting should have its own title. Consider the following examples:

- I Froze in Terror.
- I Screamed in Silence.
- I Am Alone. I Am Alone.
- Emptiness Surrounds Me.
- Happiness Swells within Me.
- I Won. I Won.
- I Am Weightless with Joy.
- Gaiety Is Everywhere.

Unit 2.
Painting to Music

Sounds evoke sensations for the artist that are meaningful and definable. (Figures 39, 40)

The realization is made that the world of music uses the medium of sound to convey its expressions while the world of art uses the visual medium to express similar values. Vibrating, rhythmical sounds penetrate the senses and stir up imagery that can be interpreted in painting. The task for the student is to make sensitive translations from what is heard to what is seen.

Painting Activity

Preparation for the lesson: start with a selection from a specific musical theme. The choice can be made from one of the three approaches suggested here.

Classical music. This area affords considerable resources for motivation. Within its sphere can be found musical compositions which evoke images that are enchanting, exotic, fantastic, magical, mysterious.

Popular music. Select contemporary music that has immediate appeal, such as folk, jazz, popular, ethnic. A recorder may be used to tape pertinent segments in order to control the development and transition of select musical sounds.

Tape sounds originating from everyday experiences. Control their loudness and intensities. Combine ordinary and unusual sounds to create exaggerated rhythms and unexpected inflections.

Begin the painting activity: listen to musical sounds that are brassy, melodic, lyrical, or filled with emotion. Discover that musical themes have subtle or sudden changes in the tempo of sound and movement. Hear and feel expressions in music, and, in turn, interpret them in terms of painting. See imagery or explosive outbursts of color or gentle undulating lines and shapes that describe the sounds which travel through the atmosphere. Create a painting that reveals what is heard and imagined.

The air is filled with music the entire time the painting is evolved and completed.

40. Response to Musical Sounds

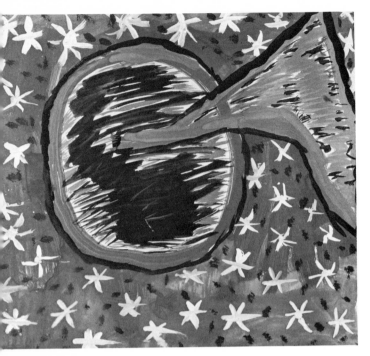

Unit 3.
Interpretation Through Design

The understanding of a poem or story will lead to sensitive, original interpretations. (Figures 41-43)

The written word challenges our intellect to undertake a process of thinking that provokes our senses. Ideas and imagery become lasting through the written word, which can then be communicated beyond the barriers of distance and time. The introduction of select passages from poetry and literature as the framework for creative expression will show the student that, like painting, written statements transmit the feelings and beliefs of man as well as reflect his search for knowledge and truth.

41, 42. Two Interpretations: Poem by Rachel Brody, *Silence*

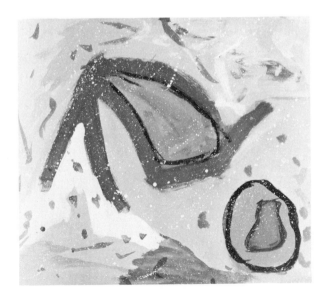

43. Interpretation: Poem by Robert Frost, *Fire and Ice*

Painting Activity

Poetry. Poetic verses impart ideas and experiences that are imaginative, reflective, and passionate, charmed with the element of surprise. Poems arouse personal responses; they stimulate visions and imagery; they elicit exceptional concepts and viewpoints; they create statements of whimsy or fun and fancy.

Select a poem that highlights visual images, intensifies color sensations, and fosters a mood or atmosphere. Discuss it, and determine the key words or phrases that disclose the ideas of the author. Make a painting that translates in a personal manner the ideas stated.

Story. Select passages from stories on the students' reading list. Or compose an original short story, considering such topics as:

- Water as a Way of Life or as a Source of Amusement.
- Which Door to a Strange World: the Red, Yellow, or Blue?
- Fire Conquers Man as Man Conquers Fire.

Interpret the significance of the key passages through the use of color, composition, and subject matter. Create the general mood of the literary work. Give a personal interpretation in the painting.

Unit 4.
Imagination and Invention

Personal inner visions impart creative descriptions. (Figures 44, 45, Color la, lb, lc)

Here, ideas that originate from within the student are communicated. The expression of thoughts

44. Imagination and Invention: Green People

that may wander from what is mundane is respected and made colorful through originality and fancifulness. The student is shown that the substance of personal notions can be put forth with clarity in a painting.

Painting Activity

Everyone has imagination. This can be defined as the inner vision of creativity. That which is imaginative is an exaggeration of the real world. That which is imaginary is the creation of something that never existed and becomes the world of fancy, make-believe, unreality.

45. Imagination and Invention: The Dragon That Flew

Unit 5.
Discovering Subject Matter in Design

Subject matter can be identified in an imaginative way. (Figures 46-49)

By allowing ourselves the luxury to see things that are not really there, we can discover many wondrous forms derived from what is real. Their relation to subject matter is assured by the addition of details that identify specific motifs. The student is encouraged to rely upon his knowledge of what exists to help him define images in an inventive way.

Everyone can be inventive. This occurs when imagination and reality are combined to transform what is ordinary to appear different, mysterious, and unusual. Through imagination and inventiveness we can express in a painting strange, dreamlike worlds. Broad vistas of unexplored and enchanting realms can be made vivid and given explicit form.

Consider topics from which one can embark into the land of fantasy and invention:
- Enchanted Forest of the Mini-People.
- Nature's Way on a Distant Planet.
- A Journey Among the Eerie Creatures of the Deep Sea.
- Fabulous Monsters Roam in My Dreamland.
- My World Is Seen Through a Kaleidoscope.
- Time Machine into the Past or Future.

Remember that important aspects to effective expression of an imaginative scene include original interpretation of subject matter, unexpected use of colors, and unity in the overall arrangement of the design elements in the painting.

46. Discovery: A Snail

47. Discovery: A Flower

48. Discovery: An Elephant

49. Discovery: A Dragon

Painting Activity

Select several colors, and begin to produce a painting, applying concepts of design previously learned. When it is partially completed, stop and look at the painting. Turn the paper sideways or upside down. Use imagination, be inventive, and discover shapes within the painting that remind one of familiar forms. Can you discover subject matter such as a bird, a ship, a flower, an animal, a strange creature?

As the painting is completed, clarify the recognizable form through the use of strong outlines. Add details or accents of color to emphasize its shape. Modify and contrast the areas surrounding the recognizable form to make the subject matter become the center of interest in the painting.

Unit 6.
Atmosphere of a Scene

The mood of a scene pervades its atmosphere. (Figures 50-52)

Common views of our environment take on new conditions when we regard their attributes. The student is led to become alert to and appreciate the many moods of his surroundings. He makes the discovery that his environment is colored by diverse features and activities, and its appearance is modified by natural phenomena. The student will then be able to depict a scene filled with mystery and drama, further enhanced by his personal perception.

50. Atmosphere: Thunderstorm in the Night

51. Atmosphere: Darkness and Snow

52. Atmosphere: A Moment of Solitude

Painting Activity

Describe the essential qualities of the two words "atmosphere" and "scene." Be specific.

Atmosphere: the mass of air that surrounds all things. Its mood can be serene, noisy, eerie, thunderous, lively, still, foreboding.

Scene: the single view of what is in sight. It can include city skyscrapers, ocean seaport, wide desert, mountain ranges, animal farm, large factories, dense forest.

Consider a specific setting within a larger scene that can be adapted for a painting. Simplify and emphasize aspects of the scene to enrich and strengthen its composition. Fill the painting with colors that harmonize with the mood.

Suggested topics:
- Nightfall over the gray, restless city.
- Serene, breezy forest at sunset.
- Bustling seaport stirring with ships.
- Noisy, busy, clattering factories.
- Awesome, misty-top mountains.
- Sunrise over the tranquil seacoast.

Unit 7.
Painting a Theme in Design

53. A Building Is on Fire!
54. Mask of Carnival Fun

A theme is dramatized to reveal its essential characteristics. (Figures 53-55)

General subjects often observed by the student are here studied. What is sought for are details fundamental to the subject matter under consideration which tend toward inspiring unusual compositions. When the distinctive elements are properly identified, they will bring about illustrations of the themes chosen which are rich with description and interpretation.

Painting Activity
Themes that generate immediate interest and attention include the amusement park, the circus, construction and demolition of buildings, harvest time, the fishing fleet, the airport.

Select one theme; seek out and identify its important characteristics to stimulate meaningful ways of interpreting the subject. The theme chosen for a painting is made more significant when the following points are carefully considered:

• There are specific types of activities and actions found in a given theme.
• There is an unfolding sense of drama that heightens the spirit of the theme.
• Subject matter found within the theme can be rendered with a new viewpoint.

As the painting is brought to completion, give special attention to details that convey the flavor of the theme, such as its excitement, its fun, its suspense, its activity.

55. Boardwalk in the Wintertime

Unit 8.
Imaginative Points of View

What is familiar can be enhanced through new ways of seeing. (Figures 56, 57)

There are many ways of seeing what is familiar. It can be observed that as we walk past a familiar scene, new facades come into view, while others gradually fade from our line of vision. As one advances toward the scene, details previously unnoticed become distinct and sometimes appear impressively prominent.

The level of vision can be changed to produce compositions that are exceptional and surprising. Select a high position—atop a building, a bridge, a hill—and look down upon the broad vista, or,

56. Distant View of the City Harbor

57. Closeup View of the Ferris Wheel

from a lower level, glance up towards the uppermost limits of the vista. See that vertical and curved lines appear to turn obliquely; see that flat, horizontal planes shift direction to create a sensation of movement in depth.

New visual statements of what is familiar can be achieved in a painting. Select specific features within a setting, and view them in a personal way to create a singular composition.

Suggested topics:
- Looking down upon the wide expanse of my environment (wide open fields, meandering rivers, city rooftops).
- Patterns and textures denote the facades of my environment (brick, wood, metal, glass, water).
- Imposing architectural details are found in my environment (bridge, house, water tower, railroad depot).

5 Human Figures in Painting

Man and his activities are central to our world and to our daily experiences. Everything we see, everything we do discloses the presence of man and his relationships with other people. We live in the world of man; we are affected by the actions of man; we are involved with the affairs of man.

With regard to the subject of man as the motif to be expressed in painting, we recognize that the older student may tend to shy away from representing the human figure. This is due to the uncertainty of his own ability to make visual statements that are acceptable. Therefore, this chapter introduces basic techniques for illustrating the human figure that will bring confidence to the student without burdening him with technical knowledge in anatomy. He will then be able to evolve a personal style of depicting the human figure, while exploring the many ways in which the human figure can be described in expressive settings, displaying a variety of poses and situations.

Unit 1.
Human Structure

There is a basic relationship among the parts of the human form. (Figure 58)

In this first exercise, have the student analyze and discover for himself that the parts of the human figure are interrelated in a way that remains constant. Show that details of the human form can be reduced to simplified lines and shapes which appear convincing. Demonstrate how body movements can be achieved by altering the position of an arm or leg.

Painting Activity
Select a student, and have him stand at attention in full view. Observe him, and undertake visual measurements, using the head as the unit of measure. Determine the height of the student according to "head-lengths." Generally, the hu-

man figure can be measured as six head-lengths: head, one head-length; shoulder to waist, two head-lengths; waist to knee, one-and-one-half head-lengths; knee to base of feet, one-and-one-half head-lengths.

Make further observations. The human figure can be divided into two parts with an imaginary line that extends down the center of the face through the body. This is a symmetrical division. Note that the relationship of one part of the body

58. The Human Figure

to another is constant. This is known as proportion. Thus, whether a human figure is drawn small or large, its proportion will remain the same. See that the elbow is aligned with the waist and that the movement of the arms follows a curved path.

Select a color, and, using simple, broad lines, begin to sketch the outline of the human figure upon the paper. Make measurements to determine how the human figure should be formed according to head-lengths. Form the limbs by relying upon direct observation. Simplify the body structure, and omit all unnecessary details.

Make a second human figure larger in size. Vary its pose by changing the position of one or two arms. Outline a third figure which displays variation in pose and size.

Fill in each human figure with flat areas of pure and mixed colors. Avoid details such as facial features or accents of clothing. Paint in the background. Now observe that the human figures have solidity and seem convincing in proportion and movement.

Unit 2.
Observed Single Poses

Different views of the human figure can be stated simply and effectively. (Figure 59)

We continue to examine the human figure from new points of view. Through direct observation the student will find that as the person turns, new aspects of the human form are seen, while others disappear from the line of vision. Further observations will enable the student to make descriptions of the human figure in a variety of action-type poses that are made plausible by tilting the body and modifying the position of the limbs.

Painting Activity

Select a student, and have him pose turned in side view. Notice that the proportion of the human figure remains the same. Make important observations concerning such questions as:

• Are both shoulders and arms visible?
• Are there any differences in the width of the body between the full view and side view of the human figure?

Have the posed student move and then freeze in mid-action. Make important observations concerning actions such as walking, bending, running. Determine the essential changes in these poses as they affect the position of the arms, feet, and back of the torso. Become aware that the movements of the elbows, knees, and feet follow a parallel curved path.

Have the posed student turn away from the observer. Make distinctions between the back view and the front view of the posed student.

Through observation, paint upon the paper the figure posed in various views, using simple contour lines. When necessary, measure with the "eyes" to ascertain the basic divisions of the human figure. The posed individual may lift one arm, bend down to touch the ground, take a step upward, or sit with arms at rest. Attempt to render these actions with assurance, relying upon direct observation and knowledge of proportion. Remember to select only the essential contours that describe the pose of the person.

Fill in each drawn figure with flat areas. Paint in the background in a manner that does not detract from the importance of the human figure.

59. Varied Poses

60. Posed Figures
in a Close Grouping

Unit 3.
Figure Grouping

Group arrangement of human figures can be made impressive. (Figures 60, 61)

In this section the human figure is no longer treated as an isolated phenomenon but is combined with several others to make a grouping. It may be shown that when each human figure is distributed with a concern for its relationship to other human figures, the group appearance will be more convincing. Thus, an impression of distance between human figures can be conveyed by placing each figure on a different groundline. One person may appear near; another may seem to be located in the background; and still another may become partly hidden in a close grouping.

Painting Activity

Select three persons, and pose them side by side. See that each of them can be viewed in his entirety. Note that the feet rest upon an imaginary horizontal line, defined as the groundline. Place one individual forward and another one farther back. See that the three persons no longer appear side by side; their feet rest on different groundlines. Now, arrange the three persons in a close grouping. See that one or more of them is partially hidden by the one standing in front. Vary the arrangement of the group so that they are lined up directly behind one another. See that the farther back an individual is, the less he is visible.

Part A. Translate what has been observed onto the flat surface of the paper. Try the following method: each time a human figure is drawn, use a different color to identify each one readily. Block in the first posed human figure somewhere toward the center of the paper. The broad outlines of the second posed figure should be placed near the first. When painting the third posed human figure, make certain that part of it is drawn partially over another human figure. In brief, one human figure must overlap another one. Before filling in the human figures with color, determine which of the overlapped figures should appear closer to the observer. This one will be seen in its entirety, while the other one will remain partially hidden.

Part B. Start again. This time include as many as five or six human figures within the grouping. Overlap as many as possible to produce a close arrangement. Vary their size so that some will appear small, while others will increase to touch the top or bottom of the paper. Alter the poses and views of the human figures to introduce a variety of actions.

Complete the painting. Add details to give individuality to the human figures. When the painting is completed, observe how the figure grouping appears to be full of movement and excitement.

61. Group Arrangement of Single Posed Figures

Unit 4.
Human Figures in a Setting

Posed human figures can be placed in a specific setting to increase the significance of their actions. (Figures 62-64)

This exercise guides the student to make a connection between the actions of human figures and the setting in which they are placed. The introduction of a well-defined background can provide a convincing appearance to the human figures in poses of movement. The selection of particular scenery will be suggested by the postures of the human figures.

Painting Activity

Have a student think of an activity, begin to perform it, and then freeze in mid-action. Try to imagine what activity has been recaptured in the frozen pose. Next, select two students, and have them stand, sit, or bend in different poses. Looking at them, attempt to place their posed movements in a single, related activity.

Apply this approach in a painting. Working

62 *(left).* Posed Figure Is My Teacher

63 *(below).* Crowds Facing Horizon

64. Posed Figures Ascending Hill

directly with paints, sketch several posed human figures upon the paper, each one drawn separately. As each posed figure is outlined, try to anticipate what activity is to be recaptured and depicted. This will determine the size and placement of each human figure in relation to each other and its importance to the composition. Continue, and finish the painting in the following manner:

- Modify the poses to stress a definite action.
- Particularize each figure to increase its individuality by introducing details of clothing and other attributes related to the activity.
- Relate the background to the human figures by including a specific setting which will emphasize the actions of the grouped figures.
- Pay attention to the selection of colors as a means to heighten the spirit of the activity.

Unit 5.
Human Figures in Activities

Action poses stress a variety of possible types of figure movements. (Figures 65-74)

Through effort and practice, man is capable of achieving unusual physical feats. Urge the student to recall instances of marvelous actions that have been observed by him and that he is able to describe. Lead him to learn that the spirit of movement is heightened by an interaction of physical tension and relaxation, particularly during those times which require the participation of numbers of people. His recollections and learnings related to human actions may be described in a painting filled with human activity.

Painting Activity
The activities of man are basic: he stands; he walks; he sits; he runs; he lies at rest. Man can train and regulate his limbs to achieve feats that might otherwise seem insurmountable. Thus he can accomplish remarkable actions: he can leap high above the ground; he can swim in the depths of the sea; he can walk in the vacuum of space.

There are infinite variations of actions that man

65. Children Playing Games

66. Horseback Rider

67. Ice Skating on a Lake

68 *(right)*. Soccer Players

69 *(below)*. Football: Running for the Touchdown

70·*(below right)*. Advancing with the Football

71. Skiers

undertakes as he moves through his world. Many actions are casually experienced and can be identified as activities. Other actions require concentrated effort. These are organized activities and can often be termed sports. Sometimes activities and sports involve the participation of two, three, or more people.

The completion of an action may require an individual to turn, twist, or stretch his limbs. He may be required to compress his body by bending or crouching, or he may extend his body by leaping upward and forward. Try to recall a frequently observed activity or sport, and attempt to depict the movements of the particular human action

65

72. Ice Hockey: Shooting to Score

73. The Discus Thrower

that best characterize the activity or sport. Focus attention upon the following considerations:

- Increase tension and suspense by dramatizing the highlights of the action.
- Display the involvement of several persons by interrelating the actions of each individual within the group.
- Introduce the element of surprise by depicting unexpected activities or figure motions.

74. Gymnastic Exercises

Unit 6.
Themes Emphasizing
the Human Figure

Themes convey a concern for human participation in a given environment. (Figures 75-80, Color II)

There are themes which highlight man's involvement with his surroundings. The extent to which man is obliged to rely upon his environment can be defined by such expressions as temporary, enduring, complex, casual. Once the student has pursued one or more of such themes, he will gain a deeper understanding of the scope of man's activities with their dependence upon a particular environment. This understanding will be reflected in his painting.

Painting Activity
Consider themes which emphasize the importance of the human figure and, at the same time, generate new approaches for considering man as part of the totality of his environment. Notice

75. Busy Thoroughfare

76. Bicycle Riders   77 *(facing page)*. Construction Workers

IIIa. City Sunset.
Painting by 14-year-old boy.

IIIb. Bird and Nest.
Painting by 13-year-old girl.

78. Clown Performers

that man's relationship to a particular environment may be placed on different levels. For example, man's contact with his surroundings may be permanent, and, therefore, his environment becomes a way of life. Man may have an occasional contact with a specific surrounding, which makes the relationship casual. A particular environment may be the source of fun or pain or fear, a relationship that is sought for or shunned by man.

Select themes for a painting, such as: man and the sea, circus performers, rush-hour crowds, the big parade, man and his occupation. Determine the many aspects in which the theme can be presented in an original manner, making the human figure the center of interest. Give attention to:

- The point of vision in the depiction of the theme.
- The stressing of a specific phase of the theme.
- The use of color and line to suggest the mood and quality of the theme.
- Creating interest and movement through variety of human actions.
- The selection and arrangement of light and dark areas to produce a dramatic effect.

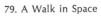

79. A Walk in Space

80. The Newlyweds

Unit 7.
Self-Portrait

81. Self-Portrait: As I See Myself

A portrait expresses the mood, character, and personality of the person. (Figures 81-87, Color IVb)

The individuality of a person is depicted in a portrait. An image can reveal qualities that describe the physical attributes and distinctive traits of the person. We limit the topic of portraiture for the student; a portrait should be the description of a real person known best to the student—himself. The making of a self-portrait will arouse a serious effort to know more about oneself. It will give the student courage to analyze himself and to depict his image in a purposeful way.

Later, this unit may be expanded to include individuals known by the student—members of his family, friends, neighbors, teachers.

Painting Activity

Consider the external characteristics of the self-portrait:

- The individual can represent himself in full, profile, or three-quarter view.
- He can strive for a precise rendering of his physical features. Or he can elaborate upon those features that enhance the singleness of the person—the hair, the lines of the eyebrows, eyes, and mouth, the structure of the nose, the skin tones.
- He can exaggerate one or more physical attributes which will lead to caricature.

82 *(facing page)*, 83 *(above)*, 84 *(right)*.
Self-Portraits: As I See Myself

85 (facing page), 86 (above), 87 (above right).
Self-Portraits: As I See Myself

Consider the intrinsic characteristics of the self-portrait:

- The individual can present those qualities that best describe his inner feelings and attitudes about himself. He can impart what he considers essential to the identity of the self.

- Facial features can be treated as a series of related planes and surfaces with the addition of details to provide emphasis of individuality.
- Reliance upon the role of colors can be made to bring out the mood or feeling of the self.
- The use of strong, hard contours or soft lines and the gradation of shadows or sharp contrasts can enlarge the penetration of inner depth and revelation of the self-portrait.

6 Nature

In this section we turn to the natural world.

The world we live in is filled with many strange, exciting vistas and living creatures that affect our lives directly and indirectly. Throughout human history, there has been a continuous struggle to bring the forces of nature under the will of mankind. Man, when he failed to understand its significance, brought waste and destruction upon nature. When man's knowledge taught him to appreciate its full power, he utilized his energies to protect and sustain nature. Accompanying this effort is the realization that nature possesses a life of its own which must always be respected. Moreover, the forces of nature are not constant but in a state of continuous change, and these forces can hinder or improve the well-being of mankind.

To develop a greater awareness and appreciation for the multi-faceted character of nature, a series of planned topics for painting activities is given. This area of study is intended to increase the student's sensitivity to his immediate environment by providing opportunities to give it expression through painting. Beyond this, he will be led to gain insight into the vaster natural world, which he may have only glimpsed or perhaps never seen and only imagined.

Unit 1.
Landscapes and Seascapes

Qualities of a landscape or seascape yield sights of spaciousness and vividness. (Figures 88-90)

The characteristics of nature are investigated, with consideration given primarily to its physical traits. Have the student realize that there is a variety of color, pattern, texture, and subject matter in the view of nature. Show that nature is animated with rich, harmonious hues that remain unsurpassed and that it abounds with surface patterns and textures that need to be discovered, studied, and described to be fully appreciated.

Painting Activity
The view of nature is animated. We move through its vast domain and observe its infinite variety of displays. In a state of continuous change

88. Row of Trees

89. Mountain Range

90. Freighter upon the Open Sea

are nature's physical forms, which emerge, develop, alter, erode, disappear, and come forth again.

Select a segment of nature and portray its important characteristics in a planned composition. Focus attention upon elements of nature whose subject matter includes:

Landscape. It consists of a horizon separating land and sky. The horizon becomes a contour that defines mountains, rivers, valleys, deserts, forests. The land may be seen in its natural state, untouched and rugged, or it is found to be cultivated, producing a refinement of features.

Seascape. It consists of a horizon separating sea and sky. The horizon becomes a contour that defines ocean waves, irregular shorelines, sandy beaches, rocky cliffs.

Enrich and strengthen the interpretation of a landscape or seascape by defining such qualities as the sense of distance and space, the sense of movement, the sense of timeliness.

Unit 2.
Cityscapes

The special character of a city transforms the appearance of the natural environment. (Figures 91-93, Color IIIa)

Man lives in the world of nature. To satisfy personal needs, man has built into the natural world villages, towns, and cities. These are frequently

80

so grand in size that they overpower our ability to view them in their entirety. The student's familiarity with his own, immediate environment can initiate this topic of study. Guide him from what is generally seen and oftentimes only partially understood to a greater knowledge and appreciation of the features that constitute the man-made world.

91. Highway Leading into the City

92. The Bridge

93. City at Night

Painting Activity

The view of the city has fascination. Become aware of its distinctive traits. See that it is the achievement of man's continuous effort to manipulate nature to satisfy personal needs.

Select a segment of the city, and depict its principal features through the use of subject matter, color, and composition. Consider the appearance of the city, whose subject matter includes: a horizon comprising irregularly drawn structures separating land and sky; tightly woven patterns of edifices made from stone, glass, concrete, and steel; waterfronts filled with ships and boats of all kinds; impressive bridges.

Enrich and strengthen the interpretation of a cityscape by defining such qualities as the sense of awe and power through monumental size, the sense of energetic change through construction and demolition, the sense of familiarity through the addition of details.

Unit 3.
Nature's Seasons

The character of a scene is affected and modified by the seasons of the year. (Figures 94-97)

This unit stresses the ways in which natural features alter with the seasons. It is convenient to start with an analysis of each of the seasons—spring, summer, autumn, winter. Have the student take notice of the means by which the seasons modify land-, sea-, and cityscapes, which include the elements of color, atmosphere, and weather. There are many possibilities for interpreting the topic through painting, ranging from broad vistas to specific details that highlight the spirit of the season.

94. Springtime

Painting Activity

Through nature's way, landscapes are transformed and re-created into new visual experiences. These changes occur during the four seasons—winter, spring, summer, autumn. Sometimes there is a gradual transition from one season to another. Other times it is sudden and unexpected. Recall what constitutes the attributes of each season. Imagine how a specific landscape setting may appear during different seasons. Think how a particular season of the year will affect the hues, mood, and detail views of a scene.

Select a landscape scene during a season of the year. Dramatize its principal qualities by interpreting and using, as a point of departure, one topic from among a select list, such as:

- An autumn sunset.
- Leaves falling from a tree.
- Snow on the bridge.
- Blossoms peek forth.
- Shadows upon the earth.
- Reflections in the puddle.
- Raindrops against the glass.
- Glaring sun upon the wide terrain.

95. Desert in Summer

96. Autumn Haystacks

97. City Snowfall

Unit 4.
Plant Life

The natural world is brilliant with thriving plant life. (Figures 98-100)

In this section, the student is directed to look closer at the plants which give nature its beauty and life. Vegetation of all kinds, whether grown in a natural state or carefully cultivated, is the subject for special consideration. A study of plants and flowers will suggest that vegetation is remarkable for its infinite variety of line and structure, of color and design, of strength and delicacy. These qualities of plant life deserve to be expressed in a painting.

Painting Activity

Plant life varies in size and shape. It grows tall as a tree; it twists as a vine; it spreads outward as a blossoming leaf. In the life of a plant there is a delicate balance of beauty and growth that leads to a moment of perfection.

98. Flowers in Bloom

IVa. Abstraction. Painting by 12-year-old boy.

IVb. Self-Portrait. Painting by 15-year-old boy.

99. Potted Plant

Look at a leaf. Investigate its surfaces. Note how precise and intricate is the pattern that it forms. Follow the contour, and see whether it is jagged, rounded, irregular, or symmetrical.

Look at a flower. Analyze its main parts: it has a stem, leaves, and petals. Compare it with another flower. Seek out the differences in appearance.

See the infinite variety of color that covers plant life. Observe its deep, intense hue, and follow the subtle changes of color resulting from light and shadow. Translate in a painting the fantasy of floral and plant life. Be imaginative, and create a part of nature that bursts with color, vitality, and inspiration.

100. The Garden

Unit 5.
Animal Life

The animal world teems with living creatures that fascinate and amaze. (Figures 101-103, Color IIIb)

This area focuses upon the infinite variety of living creatures that inhabit the natural world. An orderly approach to this study is first to distinguish the broad categories in which fauna are placed: animal, bird, fish, insect. Once this is accomplished, proceed to have the student discover, identify, and define the many members,

that make up each of these groups. Develop within the student an awareness and appreciation of the attributes that these living creatures possess. Further distinctions may be made between fauna that are familiar to our environment and the many more that appear strange and are uncommon.

Painting Activity

Living creatures, large and small, inhabit the vast domain of the natural world. Some can soar up to the clouds; some possess the power to attain high regions with deft steps; some seek the depths of the dark seas; some hide behind dense plant growth. The world of wildlife belongs to the animals, the insects, the fishes, and the birds.

Select a specific member of wildlife, and analyze the qualities that best define its identity. Examine its attributes with regard to:

Appearance. Each living creature has definite shape and size. Individuality of type among the many families of wild life is increased through unusual color and body patterns. Descriptive qualities may include graceful, gentle, furry, soft, ferocious, mysterious, comical, exotic.

Animation. Each form of wildlife has movement peculiar to its kind. These kinds of motions can be distinguished as agile, awkward, slow, silent, sliding.

Sound. Each member of the animal world communicates with sounds that evoke responses. These tones can be described as howls, shrieks, songs, roars, whines, screeches, barks.

Do a painting that interprets in an imaginative way the characteristics of a member of wildlife. Give importance to anatomical details that individualize the living creature. Exaggerate its appearance to emphasize its distinctiveness. Provide a specific habitat.

102. Ladybug

103. Cat Hiding Behind Bush

101 *(facing page)*. Running Tiger

104. Bottles

105. Jug and Vase

Unit 6.
Still-Life

A variety of objects can be utilized to produce good still-life compositions. (Figures 104-106)

Opportunities are given to the student to probe among ordinary objects and to collect those items that stimulate personal interest. He is shown that common materials have qualties of form, pattern, texture, and volume which, once investigated, will ascertain their value as subjects for a painting. An arrangement of chosen objects will produce unusual compositions.

Painting Activity

Look about, and collect common objects that can be considered for purposes of study. Analyze several of these found objects.

Observe each one from various points of view: from above, from below, from the side. Turn each object slowly to discover unusual contours and new shapes.

Observe how light falls upon each object to create shadows. See the importance of light and shadow as a means to strengthen the appearance of three dimensions.

Group together several objects consisting of a variety of materials, such as glass, fabric, metal, wood. Compare their surface pattern and texture, their hardness, softness, or pliability of substance. See and become aware of light as it highlights and deepens hues, as it creates gradual or sudden transitions of shadows upon each object.

Select several objects, and place them in an interesting arrangement. These objects may be similar or varied in identity and shape. Develop a still-life painting that can be more meaningfully designed by regarding some of the following aspects:

- The composition may present a surprising point of view.
- A concern for the careful placement of objects can lead to a dynamic, rhythmical, or balanced composition.
- Sensitive, bold, delicate, or strong qualities can be evolved in the composition through dramatic or subtle use of light and shadow.

106 (facing page). Flowers in a Vase

7 Learning Through Visual Aids

Visual aids make painting experiences more exciting. By being integrated in painting lessons, visual aids can stimulate fresh approaches toward imaginative responses in painting. Visual aids can strengthen the validity for presenting personal ideas and developing new techniques. They can be used to introduce a cross-section of general art styles, historical periods, and attitudes revealed by artists in their works.

Visual aids are adaptable to any painting experience. The aims that should be considered when introducing visual materials come under three important categories. One category is to furnish a means to survey the theme or topic to be explored. Another is to provide specific examples related to the theme or topic under discussion. Lastly, the inclusion of visual materials can supply a range of possible approaches through which a painting may be resolved in a creative manner.

Types of Visual Aids

There are many types of visual aids, progressing from the common teaching device of chalk and board to painting demonstrations, book illustrations, filmstrips, and 16mm. films. The four types discussed below have been selected because they are teacher-controlled. They can be organized to suit the particular needs of a lesson or unit of study.

Slides. Color slides generally provide a fine quality of art reproductions. The standard equipment is the 35mm. slide projector, which can be manipulated with ease. Slides may be obtained from numerous sources, including museums and commercial companies specializing in the sale of art slides.

Postcard prints. Postcard reproductions of paintings are readily available and inexpensive. The machine which may be used for transferring the reproductions upon the screen is the opaque projector. Although the machine is large in size, it is surprisingly easy to use, and it projects the image clearly and effectively. It is suggested that the postcards be mounted on uniform white boards that have been cut slightly large in size. This ensures a stable backing and also frames the illustration nicely.

Large color prints. Unlike the above types of visual aids, large art prints can be viewed for an extended period of time under regular lighting conditions. They therefore encourage a wonderful opportunity for in-depth discussions and analyses. Two or more art reproductions can be placed side by side to make comparisons, to discover what is familiar, what is different, what is singular.

8mm. or Super 8mm. films. Painting experiences can be motivated in an animated manner. Any teacher can become a producer-director and make short movie films of 5 to 10 minutes' duration. Once the initial investment of an 8mm. camera and projector is made (the cost can be offset by the school), the rest should be fun and rewarding. Plan ahead for subjects that will inspire greater appreciation towards the theme selected for interpretation in the painting experience. The unfolding drama of the film can be made richer with the addition of a sound track. Simply play a record, or, better still, prepare and tape a sound track made especially for the film. Over a period of time, a small library of 8mm. motivation-type films will develop.